FOUNDATION FORCES

THOSE WHO SHAPED SAVANNAH

FOUNDATION FORCES

THOSE WHO SHAPED SAVANNAH

ARLENE ANGWIN

Scribe Tree Publishing

Scribe Tree Publishing

Scribe Tree Publishing, LLC

P. O. Box 196

Guyton, GA 31312

...With special thanks to Ki Coleman who always pushes me beyond what I think I can do. He had the vision of exploring the spiritual founders and shapers of Savannah. The honor of research and writing fell on me.

Your people will rebuild long-deserted ruins,
building anew on foundations laid long before you.
You will be known as Repairers of the Cities
and Restorers of Communities (Isaiah 58:10 TPT).

...And a special challenge to all who love Almighty God, true history and Savannah. The people in this book built a strong foundation of kingdom principles. Now, it is our turn to rebuild those foundations and bring back into God's original intent our city, country and the world.

By the blood of his cross, everything in heaven and earth is
brought back to himself—back to its original intent, restored to
innocence again (Colossians 1:20 TPT)!

CONTENTS

Georgia ...

The last and largest of Great Britain's 13 original colonies in North America, Georgia was founded to be a buffer between the English settlers of South Carolina and hostile Spanish of the Florida Territory. King George II had signed a charter on April 21, 1732, establishing the Georgia Board of Trustees to govern this new colony, named in his honor. Educated and influential men banded together to formulate and govern their utopian dream colony.

One of those named trustees was **James E. Oglethorpe**. In the 20 years that the board governed Georgia, he was the only one to physically go to the new land, carrying in his heart and head many definitive ideas for creating what he considered the perfect colony: No slavery, no rum, no lawyers and certainly no conflicts with Catholics, such as those pesky Spaniards in Florida. Religious persecutions and wars had dogged Europe for far too long.

Oglethorpe sailed with the first group of settlers on November 17, 1732. After stopping in Charles Town (Charleston, SC, today), the ship sailed 17 miles up the Savannah River where Oglethorpe saw a high bluff on its south side. This he chose for Georgia's first settlement. He asked a couple, John and **Mary Musgrove** — both born to Creek Indian mothers and English fathers, to serve as interpreters for negotiations with the local mico (chief), **Tomochichi**. A mutual respect sprang up between the two leaders from their first meeting, which lasted to the end of the mico's life, because both men honored every promise made.

During negotiations, Oglethorpe had requested and received the land where Savannah now sits. At once he set out to create a unique town, one laid out in multiple square grids. Homes were to line the north and south sides, while houses of worship and government buildings would face east and west. Most of this unique plan continues to this day in Savannah's two-mile historic district.

Each proposed settlement received utmost planning by Oglethorpe, with military presence at the top of his list. He began construction of Fort Frederica on St. Simon's Island, as an outpost against the Spanish-held St. Augustine. During a return trip to England, he recruited the Scots Highlanders, men renowned for their fierce fighting abilities. He directed them to settle with their families in what is now Darien, Georgia.

When the **Salzburgers**, a Germanic group from Austria fleeing Catholic persecution, arrived in 1734, he placed them northwest of Savannah to serve as a buffer against any hostile Natives and French, farther to the west.

A ship carrying 42 Jews arrived in July of 1733—unannounced, unexpected, and unwanted. Because of local prejudice, Oglethorpe hesitated to allow any to disembark. However, the moment he learned a doctor, **Samuel Nunes**, was on board, he relented. Dr. Nunes had fled to England after a new wave of inquisitions swept through his native Portugal. Now, he led a group of hopeful Jews to new life in America. Because yellow fever had swept through Savannah, threatening to wipe out his fledgling colony, Oglethorpe ignored the Georgia Trustee's stipulation of not allowing Jews in the new colony. He offered asylum to Dr. Nunes and his people, provided the doctor agreed to tend to the ill. The doctor's success delighted him so much he issued all the Jews land allotments, completely ignoring the board of trustees' express directions not to do so.

The first **Moravians** arrived in 1735. Persecuted for their religious beliefs in Bohemia (Czech Republic today) they had found refuge on Count Zinzendorf's property in eastern Germany. There, they had developed a community, Herrnhut (The Lord's House), and practiced lives of prayer, productivity, humility, and service. With a strong desire to carry the good news of Jesus throughout the known world, they had turned their attention toward America's Native peoples. Count Zinzendorf negotiated with the Georgia Board of Trustees for passage to the colonies. The first group settled in Pennsylvania while the second ship sailed to Georgia.

Savannah welcomed the industrious Moravians. They appreciated their work ethic, honesty and cheerful demeanor. However, as hostilities escalated between Spain and England, the pacifist Moravians fell out of favor for refusing to bear arms. After a stay of only five years, they joined their brothers in Quaker-friendly Pennsylvania.

Oglethorpe cared deeply about the spiritual wellbeing of his settlers. After his first return home to England, he invited his friends, **John** and **Charles Wesley**, to come and serve in Georgia. The eager young priests arrived in early 1736. John Wesley published the first hymnal in America, after translating numerous German songs, and began Savannah's first Sunday school. However, both brothers had returned to England before a year had passed.

Following their return, both men encountered God in a new manner, finally understanding through Martin Luther's teachings that salvation is by God's grace alone and cannot be earned through any good works. Their revolutionary conversions turned the British Isles upside down. For the next 50 years, as itinerant ministers, they traveled by horseback to meet and preach anywhere and everywhere. Thousands flocked to hear their message. Although severely persecuted, John Wesley persisted, preaching to the very ones he had once despised; the common folk.

Both brothers had invited their friend, **George Whitefield**, to join them in America. He sailed just before John Wesley's return to England, launching a preaching career that endured the next 30 years—in America and the British Isles. His revolutionary style of theatrics, at a time when all clergy dryly read their sermons, attracted crowds up to 25,000.

George Whitefield firmly believed America was especially chosen by God to give hope to the rest of the world. He traveled up and down the eastern seaboard numerous times, often referring to the colonies as a *Beacon on a Hill*. Although he died in 1770, he had ignited a fire that united the colonists enough to propel them into a war for freedom.

That war, the American Revolution, brought three slaves together in Savannah. All three preached freedom of spirit and soul to their enslaved brothers and sisters. **George Liele**, whose owner had freed him, sailed to Jamaica after the war and established two Baptist churches there. **David George**, who the British freed, sailed to Nova Scotia with other Black Loyalists. Later, many of those same loyalists sailed on to Sierra Leone. While his fellow Gospel laborers chose the escapes the Crown offered, **Andrew Bryan** decided to remain in Savannah to continue leading the enslaved believers there. Later, after purchasing his freedom, he bought other slaves, allowing them to work off their purchase price and become free themselves. Both George Liele and Andrew Bryan served as pastors of the First African Baptist Church, located on Franklin Square in Savannah.

Georgia. From her infancy, has enjoyed a diversity of cultures, vibrant leaders, and colonists with a strong will to survive and prosper.

PART 1

THE NEGOTIATORS

*"I am a red man, an Indian in my heart,
that is why I love them."*

—JAMES OGLETHORPE
(1696 –1785)

CHAPTER 1

JAMES OGLETHORPE

James Oglethorpe was a military leader and social reformer who had gained a reputation as a champion of the oppressed in England. He is best known for establishing the colony of Georgia in America primarily due to his desire to create a refuge for the oppressed.

The youngest of 10 children, Oglethorpe was born in London on December 22, 1696. Unfortunately, his father died when he was only 6 years old. He enrolled at Corpus Christi College in Oxford, following family tradition, but quit to go into the military. He served under Prince Eugene of Savoy, one of the most talented generals of that era. After participating in the siege of Belgrade (1717) in which the Ottomans were decisively defeated, Oglethorpe returned home.

Oglethorpe was elected to the House of Commons in 1722. He actively served on many committees, including one for prison reform. Those who failed to pay taxes or other debt found themselves behind the walls of antiquated prisons with inhumane conditions. Families of the debtor, already impoverished, were expected to supply all the debtor's needs, including food, which only deepened their distress.

Robert Castell, a talented architect and close friend of Oglethorpe, was seized after failing to pay his book publisher. He landed in Fleet Street prison, one of the most dire of all London's debtor prisons. The new warden, Thomas Bambridge, ruled with a heavy and sadistic hand. He threw Castell into a cell already occupied by a smallpox infected inmate. Castell contracted the disease and died.

The horror of his loss sent Oglethorpe on a crusade for all hapless persons so incarcerated. He discovered whole families living in the prison, simply for lack of shelter elsewhere. The debtor could only obtain freedom by paying what he owed as well as fees for the incarceration, creating an impossible situation the elite of London cared little about. Debt grew, erasing any hope of freedom.

After inspecting Fleet, and other prisons, Oglethorpe led the charge for prison reform. As awareness and talk grew, Oglethorpe became widely known. At last, horrified by the truth of debtor prison conditions, officials arrested Bambridge and put him on trial. Oglethorpe served as the main inquisitor. Bambridge was found guilty of many abuses, including murder, and sent to prison at Newgate. After his legal success over such a tyrant, Oglethorpe began dreaming of a place where those he referred to as the "deserving poor" could regain financial stability. As others expressed interest, Oglethorpe approached the king. In 1732, King George II issued a charter for the Georgia Board of Trustees, which consisted of 21 men, including Oglethorpe. The new colony, Georgia, would be settled by debtors.

> *After inspecting Fleet, and other prisons, Oglethorpe led the charge for prison reform.*

However, before plans could fully develop, The Georgia Board realized South Carolina needed protection from the Spanish in the Florida Territory, forcing Oglethorpe to change his plans. Rather than offering hope to England's debtors, he recruited skilled artisans, farmers, and merchants to quickly build a solid settlement.

On November 17, 1732, Oglethorpe, along with the chosen families, set sail from Gravesend, England to the region that presently comprises the state of Georgia. Among the cargo were supplies to produce silk and wine in their new land. The *Anne* dropped anchor on the Savannah River on February 12, 1733. He sent word of his arrival to South Carolina trader John Musgrove, Jr. and his wife Mary. He had met the couple in Charles Town and asked them to assist in talks with Tomochichi, chief of the Yamacraw Indians. Mary and John Musgrove were skilled interpreters who used their mixed English and Creek Indian heritage to more effectively assist with negotiations.

> *Despair rose in Oglethorpe's heart as colonists succumbed to the oppressive elements.*

Though Oglethorpe possessed no title from the Georgia Board of Trustees, he soon found himself as acting governor, military leader, and negotiator. He respected Tomochichi as the local mico, treating the Native ruler as a head of state. Through the Musgroves' interpretation efforts, the two leaders settled on a treaty fair to both English and Native. At its conclusion, they exchanged customary gifts. Tomochichi presented Oglethorpe with a buffalo skin, on which had been painted an eagle's head and feathers. Oglethorpe gave the old chief European clothing, gun powder, tobacco, and pipes.

Decades earlier Spanish explorer Hernando de Soto had tried to enslave the Creek Indian tribes, so the Natives trusted English traders over Spanish even though the English often cheated them through unfair trade rates. Oglethorpe promised Tomochichi fair rates in exchange for the land on which Savannah now sits. Tall pines crashed to sandy soil as men cleared land for settling.

Low country climate, however, proved deadly to the English. Heavy humidity, extreme heat and scarce clean water proved perfect conditions for disease and death. Despair rose in Oglethorpe's heart as colonists succumbed to the oppressive elements. Dr. Nunes arrived five months later, in time to combat the yellow fever and save the town.

Oglethorpe decided to return to England after only one year in Georgia, to report to the Georgia Board of Trustees in person.

He invited Tomochichi to accompany him, trusting the old mico's presence would surely help obtain necessary funds for the colony's unique needs. Privately, he knew a display of England's full power would help the chief keep the Native peoples in a position of peace. Both plans met with great success.

Shortly after Oglethorpe's return to Georgia, he and Tomochichi traveled south to scout the land. They repeated the journey in 1738, traveling to Fort Frederica, as reports of Spanish preparations for invasion came through. The old mico promised an apprehensive Oglethorpe that 1000 Creeks stood ready to fight with him. The following year, Oglethorpe traveled without Tomochichi deep into the Lower Creek territory to reinforce friendly relations between the Natives and English. Treated with great civility, he turned toward Savannah. Sorrow clouded his joy when he learned that Tomochichi had passed away during his absence.

Filled with sorrow at the loss of such a true friend, Oglethorpe ordered a military funeral for the old mico and buried the body in Percival Square (today known as Wright Square).

As the Spanish threat continued growing, Oglethorpe returned to England to explain the gravity of the situation to both the board and the crown. With permission, he sought out the Highlanders, Scotland's veterans, legendary for bravery in battle. The recruits sailed with their families and Oglethorpe to Georgia. He settled them in a strategic area, which today is known as Darien.

> *In the 10 years Oglethorpe worked to build Savannah and secure Georgia, he was both loved and hated.*

The War of Jenkins' Ear began when Captain Robert Jenkins reported to a committee from the House of Commons. During his speech, he pulled a severed ear from his coat, claiming it to be his own. He told his horrified audience that the Spaniard who had parted the ear from his head lamented that it was not the ear of King George himself. They could not ignore such an insult to their monarch and voted to declare war on Spain. Soon, hostilities spilled over into the colonies. Savannah's women and children fled to Ebenezer.

In 1742, the Spanish invaded an outer island. Oglethorpe knew he could never win against their superior numbers, so he tricked the Spaniards into thinking he had retreated. In great jubilation, the enemy army stacked arms to cook and enjoy a leisurely lunch. With their guard completely down, Oglethorpe ordered his small force to attack. The Battle of Bloody Marsh was a huge victory for the English.

In the 10 years Oglethorpe worked to build Savannah and secure Georgia, he was both loved and hated. People called him Father. He single-handedly built and ran the colony, often using his own resources to outfit soldiers when the king, the Board of Trustees and governor of South Carolina ignored his requests. Others felt he commanded too much power and accused him of dictatorial practices.

As peace settled, people turned from fear to profit. Many began grumbling against Oglethorpe's strong stance against slavery. Others spread lies of mismanagement to the Georgia Board of Trustees which ordered his recall. He left Georgia in 1743 and never returned.

Oglethorpe lived to see Americans win freedom from Great Britain before his death in 1785. Georgia owes a great deal to his dream, dedication, and perseverance. Without him, the Spanish could have easily retaken all the land from the St. Johns River to the Savannah River.

2

"When I die, I want to be buried in the white man's town and not in the forest."

—TOMOCHICHI
(1644 – 1739)

CHAPTER 2

TOMOCHICHI

Tomochichi was already an old man when Oglethorpe first met him. He had been chief of a tribe in Alabama. For unknown reasons, in 1728 he moved to the east coast, along with 200 family members and loyal followers. Tomochichi named his new tribe Yamacraw. They settled on the bluff overlooking the Savannah River.

A few years later, the Musgroves opened a trading post on the South Carolina side of the river. Shortly after their move, they visited the old mico with news of Oglethorpe's impending visit. Not long after that, they brought news of a white leader coming to negotiate.

Tomochichi met Oglethorpe with a mixture of anxiety and hope. South Carolina men had traded with neighboring tribes for years. Many behaved unethically, always seeking to cheat the Natives. More than that, settlers built homes on native property, clearing valuable hunting grounds for their livestock. Growing tension erupted into the Yamasee War (1715-1717). Frustrated Braves massacred many settlers, with traders as prime targets. Although Tomochichi's kinsmen refused to join in the fight, he remembered well the armed superiority of the British. His spirit told them the white wave of humanity would not be stopped. He understood British superiority, both in firepower and education. He saw some display religion which appeared far less barbaric than native traditions. He sensed the younger generations would face a new world completely alien to what he and all other Natives had known before. For this reason, he resolved to find a way of peace that would be fair to his people and the rising British tide.

Oglethorpe's respectful demeanor of treating the aging man as an equal won him over from the start. The mico voiced every concern while laying out his conditions for fair trade in exchange of native lands. The agreed-upon treaty brought joy to both sides. The leaders exchanged gifts amid much celebration.

A lasting kinship grew between the two men. Once, when a Native accused a White man of killing his kinsman, Tomochichi stepped between the two and bared his chest. "Start with me," he declared. "For I, too, am an Englishman." Oglethorpe showed the same fair determination when delivering justice for altercations with his own countrymen.

In 1734, when Oglethorpe asked the chief to go to England with him to meet the Georgia Trustees face to face, Tomochichi accepted with great delight. His wife, Senauki, and nephew, Toonahowie, accompanied him. Given the mico's status among the Natives, six other chiefs along with their attendants also sailed.

> *In 1734, when Oglethorpe asked the chief to go to England with him to meet the Georgia Trustees face to face, Tomochichi accepted with great delight.*

Oglethorpe asked John Musgrove to go as interpreter. When the entourage stepped ashore, Oglethorpe was the most famous man in England. Many were curious as well as excited about his Georgia experiment. The Georgia Board of Trustees provided lodging for the Natives. They quickly met to go over the terms of the treaty made the year before. A vote was taken, and the Board unanimously accepted it.

Business resolved, the Natives settled into celebrity status. British everywhere feted them. On August 1, 1734, three coaches, drawn by six horses each, arrived to present the entire entourage to the king. They were ushered into the throne room where King

George II sat with Queen Caroline by his side. Tomochichi stepped forward to deliver a speech through John Musgrove. He referred to the Articles of Commerce and Friendship he had helped negotiate and sign in 1721, expressing his everlasting desire for peace between the two peoples. He told the king he came to him as an old man, desirous of seeing the next generation of his people educated in the English ways. Then, he presented the monarch with several eagle feathers.

"These are the feathers of the eagle which is the swiftest of birds, and who flieth all round our nations. These feathers are a sign of peace in our land and have been carried from town to town there; and we have brought them over to leave with you, O great king! As a sign of everlasting peace."

The king accepted his gift with promises for continued peace. Next, the old mico turned to the queen. "I am glad to see this day and to have the opportunity of seeing the mother of this great people. As our people are joined with your Majesty's, we do humbly hope to find you the common mother and protectress of us and all our children."

The king's youngest son, William Augustus, Duke of Cumberland, was present to meet Tomochichi's heir, Toonahowie. The two were about the same age. The prince gave the native boy a gold watch and New Testament.

Three days after the audience with the king, tragedy struck. One of the chiefs had contracted smallpox. Despite the best medical care London offered, he died. While the Natives expressed grave concerns over leaving their dead brother in a foreign land, Oglethorpe persuaded them it must be so. The fallen warrior was buried in St. John's cemetery, Westminster. However, Oglethorpe ensured the burial proceeded, following native customs. After sewing the body into two blankets, the others pressed it between two boards, which they then lashed together. After lowering the native styled coffin into the grave, the mourners tossed glass beads and silver pieces into the grave. Sensitive to the Natives' grief, Oglethorpe took them all to his estate to allow private mourning for two weeks.

During their four-month stay, the Natives toured the Tower of London, Hampton Court, Eton, Greenwich Hospital and met with the Archbishop of Canterbury. Everywhere they went, people flocked to see them while Tomochichi studied the buildings, wondering why short-lived men built such long-lived structures. Before leaving Oglethorpe in England, Tomochichi told him, "I'm glad to be going home, but to part with you is like the day of death. You have never broken a promise to us. When I die, I want to be buried in the white man's town and not in the forest."

Oglethorpe returned to Georgia the following year, on February 5, 1736. With him were Salzburger refugees, the Highlander soldiers, and two Anglican priests, John and Charles Wesley. After setting the Highlanders to work cutting a road between Savannah and the Altamaha River sixty miles south, aided by Tomochichi's men as guides, the mico, his wife,

> *He buried his friend in the center of Percival Square (named for good friend and fellow Georgia Trustee).*

nephew, and attendants met with Oglethorpe aboard ship, anchored off Tybee Island. He expressed his delight in meeting the Wesleys, sent to fulfill his desire to instruct the Yamacraw children in Christianity. His wife presented the brothers with two jars, one filled with honey and the other with milk, welcoming them to Georgia and her people.

The aged mico (probably close to 100 years old) died on October 5, 1739. Upon his return, Oglethorpe ordered a full military funeral and served as pallbearer. He buried his friend in the center of Percival Square (named for good friend and fellow Georgia Trustee). Later, it was renamed Wright Square. He instructed his men to fashion a monument of piled stones, honoring native tradition, over the grave—most likely the first of its kind on

American soil. In 1883, Savannah wanted to honor W.W. Gordon, instrumental in building Georgia's first railroad. Years later, the city decided to build a monument to Gordon in the same place. No remains could be found. Nellie Gordon, the magnate's daughter-in-law, felt that although 150 years had passed since the mico's death, he needed to be remembered by the city. She contacted Stone Mountain Company in Atlanta, which sent the huge granite boulder that stands today in the corner of the same square.

—MARY GRIFFIN MUSGROVE
(ca. 1700 – 1765)

Mary Musgrove with her third husband, the Reverend Thomas Bosomworth. From Lawton
B. Evans, *First Lessons in Georgia History* (New York, American Book Co., 1913)
https://www.brooklynmuseum.org/eascfa/dinner_party/heritage_floor/mary_musgrove

Chapter 3

Mary Griffin Musgrove

Very little is known about Mary Griffin's first years, including the exact year of her birth. Her mother, a Creek Native, married the English trader, Edward Griffin. Tribal leaders often encouraged such unions to keep an eye on their European neighbors. Because traders' work kept them away for many months at a time, children were raised in the tribe of the mothers. Mary, and her younger brother, Edward, lived with their mother's people in Coweta Town on the Ocmulgee River (north of modern Macon, GA), until she was about 7 years old. At that time, their father moved both children to his home in PonPon, 30 miles west of Charles Town. More than likely, the reason for the move was the children's mother's death. In PonPon, Mary learned English, attended English school, adopted English dress and learned Christianity.

Tensions between unscrupulous traders and the Natives exploded in 1715, later called The Yamasee War. Native Braves sought and killed many settlers. Two traders had escaped a massacre and ran to surrounding towns to warn others. Because Mary's father was away on business, she and Edward fled to Charles Town. Others ignored the warnings. On Good Friday, Mary's Creek uncle led an attack on PonPon, killing between 90 and 100 traders. Word spread that in another town, all settlers were gathered into one building before the Natives torched it. The conflict ended two years later. In subsequent negotiations to end the violence, both sides agreed the Savannah River marked the new boundary between Native and English. No South Carolinian could cross to the south side, especially to raise livestock, on native hunting grounds.

Edward Griffin lost his life in the bloodbath, making both Mary and her brother orphans. As half-breeds (as they were called in that era), they hung between the two cultures for the rest of their lives. Mary married John Musgrove, another half-breed raised by his mother's tribe, when she was around 17 years old. Although illiterate, John Musgrove was highly sought out as an interpreter. The couple settled in St. Barts where John traded and raised livestock. As a symbol of growing wealth, the Musgroves bought several slaves to aid them on their holdings. Slavery was common in the native culture. When Braves brought home captives of war, the women decided which would be adopted, enslaved or executed.

The Musgroves enjoyed a prosperous life in PonPon. John moved into the planter class with Black slaves to work his land. Mary gave birth to two boys. However, after 15 contented years, the couple was asked to set up a trading post on the Savannah River for the convenience of both Natives and traders. They accepted, built a post on the Yamacraw Bluff and named it Cowpen. A few months later, they met James Oglethorpe, who requested John's assistance as interpreter between himself and Tomochichi. The

> *Tragedy struck the Musgrove home a year later. First, John died, followed shortly by their eldest son.*

following year, John Musgrove accompanied the mico's entourage to England. He returned with Jacob Mathewes, an indentured servant, to help him raise livestock.

Tragedy struck the Musgrove home a year later. First, John died, followed shortly by their eldest son. Oglethorpe had just returned from England with the Wesley brothers. John Wesley spent time with Mary to offer consolation. Mary appeared to turn fully to the Christian faith at that time, so when her remaining son died soon after, she brought his little body to Savannah by boat and asked John Wesley to officiate a European funeral. Wesley visited the trading post several times to offer spiritual comfort to Mary, who had lost her entire family so quickly.

The Creeks lived in a matriarchal society. However, Mary now lived and had prospered, in the European culture, where law dictated tail male. This meant only males could inherit property. She had lost all three males in her immediate family and feared she would now lose all her hard-earned property. Historians have speculated this was the reason for her marrying John Musgrove's servant, Jacob Mathewes.

After John Musgrove's death, Oglethorpe turned to Mary to interpret, especially as the threat of Spanish invasion increased. Although steeped in bitter sorrow, Mary answered Oglethorpe's increasing pleas. Mary and Jacob moved near Darien and built a second trading post. Both Mary's brother, Edward, and husband fought in the War of Jenkins' Ear. Her brother died in battle and her husband died of illness a short time later. The Spanish burned Mary's second post, which galvanized her relatives to join the fight. Shortly after peace settled over Georgia, Oglethorpe sailed for England. Before his departure, he gifted Mary with a diamond ring from his own hand and 200 pounds sterling for her four years of interpreting services.

Mary's third husband was a younger, ambitious clergyman who urged her to demand title to extensive parcels of land, including Cumberland Island, from the English. She insisted Tomochichi had granted her those lands, yet lacked credible witnesses. After 20 years of fighting, she settled with the English court for Cumberland Island, where she lived out the rest of her life.

PART 2

THE EVANGELISTS

4

"Light yourself on fire with passion and people will come from miles to watch you burn."

—JOHN WESLEY

JOHN WESLEY
(1703 – 1791)

CHARLES WESLEY
(1707 – 1788)

"Faith, mighty faith, the promise sees, And looks to God alone; Laughs at impossibilities, And cries it shall be done."

—CHARLES WESLEY

CHAPTER 4

JOHN AND CHARLES WESLEY

John and Charles Wesley were born at Epworth, England, to a parish priest and his strong-willed wife. Samuel Wesley occupied his days writing sermons, a book and composing music, oblivious to the physical needs of his extensive family. Susanna bore 19 or 20 children, half of which died at an early age. The others she reared in a Spartan environment, military fashion. All knew how to read by the age of 5, took their whippings without tears and took instruction on how to handle life in a non-emotional manner.

The parish house caught fire when John was 10 years old. Trapped in an upstairs bedroom with the fire raging closer, he faced certain death. Susanna's training, however, had taught him to use logic for every situation. Calmly, he opened his window and waited to be rescued. A man leapt on another man's shoulders to pull the lad to safety. This experience marked young John's life in that Susanna often told him God had plucked him as a brand from the burning [fire] (Zechariah 3:1, 2). This fact affected his decisions for the rest of his life.

Both boys felt a strong hunger for God in their college years. Charles formed a Holy Club where he, John, and a few other eager young men, including George Whitefield, sought to please God through extreme self-discipline and good works. They fasted, sometimes at the risk of death, visited the poor and the imprisoned, prayed for hours, and studied the Bible. They planned every moment of the day and held one another accountable to the rigid schedules. Other classmates mocked their efforts, calling them Methodists.

When James Oglethorpe asked the Wesley brothers to come to Georgia to meet the spiritual needs of the settlers, John Wesley jumped at the offer. He felt by laboring among the "heathen" he would further his own holiness. However, the brothers' stay in Georgia proved anything but successful. Even though John printed the first hymnbook in the colonies and started the first Sunday School in Savannah, his disdain for common folk alienated him from Savannahians almost immediately. The same held true for Charles serving in Frederica. While lecturing colonists struggling to survive a hostile world, they refused to participate in any common labor. Disgusted, Oglethorpe sent Charles back to England after only four months. John followed eight months later.

> *That last question had dogged John during his short time in Georgia.*

Back in London, both Charles and John experienced God in a new, real, and personal way. On the voyage to America, John had found the Morvaians on board both mystifying and intriguing. During a storm where even the most seasoned sailors begged God for mercy, the Wesleys included, the Moravians stood on deck to sing praises to God. Even their children stood, singing without panic or distress. After calm had returned, John approached the leader.

"Were you not afraid of dying?" he asked.

"No," the priest had answered.

"Nor your children?"

"No. None. We all knew we would immediately rise up from a watery grave to be with our Lord and Savior, Jesus Christ."

"How could you know this with such certainty?"

"You do not?"

That last question had dogged John during his short time in Georgia. Now, back in England, he decided he must find the peace the Moravians possessed. He located a group living in London, where he met Peter Böhler, who answered his many questions with assured patience.

Meanwhile, Charles had fallen ill. He grew frantic as he wrestled with his own attempts to please God into assurance of salvation, until he received the revelation that God saves through grace alone. A week later, while at a Bible Study hosted by the Moravians, John Wesley expressed that his heart became "strangely warmed". He, too, came to understand that salvation is given freely by God—that God's desire is to enjoy an intimate relationship with his creation. This radical truth lit a fire in the brothers that never faltered. For the next fifty years, they criss-crossed England, Scotland, Wales, and Ireland, preaching the free gift of God to all. The very commoners they had once eschewed, they now embraced. Soon all major churches slammed their doors against the two Anglican priest brothers. They took to the fields outside of towns, holding open air meetings and delivering spontaneous sermons. John and Charles Wesley, along with George Whitefield, spoke truth from their hearts. Many resisted. Their lives were in constant danger, yet they knew no fear. Often their very bravery saved their lives. The brothers, who once alienated people through their own religiosity, now drew crowds of thousands, who heard and embraced God's amazing message of love. These three men turned Great Britain and her colonies upside down, or rather, right side up, in the Great Awakening.

"Christ is worth all, or he is worth nothing."
—GEORGE WHITEFIELD
(1714 – 1770)

CHAPTER 5

GEORGE WHITEFIELD

In 1738, a slender, cross-eyed 25-year-old man landed in Savannah—and immediately took the colonies by storm. For the next 30 years, he preached as he traveled up and down the eastern seaboard. Businesses shut down, and thousands of people flocked for miles to hear him speak. Often he spoke to more people than the people who lived in that particular town. His oratorical prowess was legendary—his message timeless.

George Whitefield, a friend of the Wesley brothers, was born in Gloucester, England, in 1714. His father died the following year. Desperately needing a man to help her with her inn, (Gloucester's Bell Inn) and for help raising her children, Whitefield's mother remarried seven years later. The union proved disastrous, culminating in a shameful divorce six years later.

As had Susanna Wesley, Mrs. Whitefield felt her youngest child was marked by God from birth. She petitioned God to bring opportunities to George, as she lacked the means to send him to Oxford—a family tradition.

Young George loved drama. Every Sunday, he fixed his full attention on the priest's sermon. Later, at the inn, he "preached" what he'd heard to the inn's customers, often bringing them to tears with his flair for delivery. Mrs. Whitefield strengthened her resolve. She enrolled George at St. Mary de Crypt school. Here is where he felt the first stirrings of spiritual awakening. However, he was forced to leave school at age 15 to help his mother in the inn. Once home, he fell into a party lifestyle.

A former classmate told George's mother of an opportunity to attend Oxford as a servitor. Both were delighted, but soon after his arrival, he once again took up partying. Soon, he became so disillusioned that he moved to the opposite extreme. He tried to crucify flesh on his own power. He needed to please God at any cost.

One night, he dreamed he was summoned to meet God. In terror, he furthered his efforts to gain God's approval. He drew up a rigorous schedule which he followed faithfully. Around this time, He learned of the Holy Club. Whitefield saw how the members were ridiculed on campus, yet longed to meet them. When John Wesley learned of his desire, he invited George to breakfast. Whitefield joined the group. Everyone increased their efforts of self-denial and good works.

Still, George felt no peace in his spirit. He decided he must have a demon and worked harder to exorcise himself. He prayed, kneeling in the snow. He failed his classes on purpose to establish humility. He became unkempt in his appearance. He fasted so much his health failed. Still, he experienced no peace in his innermost being. In complete distress, he recalled Christ's words on the cross and cried out, "I thirst."

> *In that time, he studied the Bible to grasp the truth of justification by grace.*

Instantly, the burden lifted from his heart, but the physical damage was done. He returned home for 9 months to recuperate. In that time, he studied the Bible to grasp the truth of justification by grace. His heart burned to share this truth to others.

Whitefield had another dream shortly after his return to Oxford. In it, he found himself in a bishop's castle. The cleric handed him some coins, which clinked in his outstretched hand. Soon after this, he was summoned to the local bishop's residence. During their conversation, he asked George his age.

"Twenty-one."

"I cannot ordain you until you reach the age of 23," the man replied. "However, I wish to give you this now." He reached out to hand George several coins. "Take these to buy a particular book."

As the money landed in Whitefield's palm, he remembered the dream of his time at the bishop's residence. At once, his heart filled with understanding as he realized the depths of God's love toward him. Comprehension of such profound love propelled him for the rest of his natural life.

> *George Whitefield entered life's stage at a critical time in England's history.*

The church ordained Whitefield as a deacon a few short months later. The following Sunday, he preached his first sermon. Three hundred people came to listen. In a time when clergy wrote out their sermons beforehand and merely read them to the congregation, George's flair for drama and his powerful, expressive voice served him well. He became an instant sensation. Other priests asked him to tend to their parishes in their absence. The same enthusiasm followed him. Whitefield hid from the accolades of the people, often fleeing the pulpit to hide in his room.

George Whitefield entered life's stage at a critical time in England's history. Rampant poverty against rich opulence, depravity at every level of society, and a deep, cruel cynicism had saturated the land. People came to witness Whitefield's electrifying performance, fell under conviction and embraced the Christ he preached.

During a stay in the country, Whitefield talked to anyone he met on his daily walks. In that time, clergy never engaged in conversation with the common people. Getting to know them with their everyday struggles opened his eyes to understand a God that loved all people, rich and poor. He burned with unquenchable passion to preach to anyone, anywhere.

Meanwhile, the Wesley brothers faced their own challenges in Georgia. Several months after their arrival, Whitefield received a letter from John Wesley telling him of the many opportunities in the New World. Wesley urged George to consider coming to Georgia.

He wrote, *What if thou art the man, Mr. Whitefield?* Intrigued, George accepted the challenge and began preparing for the first trip overseas. He contacted James Oglethorpe to sail with him.

During the year-long wait, he preached in many places throughout England. Throngs turned out to listen to the slender young man. The mayor of Bristol begged him to preach to the city leaders. People rejoiced when he arrived and wept at his departure. Whitefield cared nothing for denominational barriers. He preached to anyone who cared to listen. His message never changed. God desired men to repent, embrace salvation through Christ, and experience deep intimacy with him. Nothing else mattered to Whitefield.

On December, 28, 1737, Whitefield departed for Georgia. Although still in his early twenties, he was the most discussed man in England. He used the time aboard ship to preach to the passengers and crew on board. The ship arrived on May 7, to a town staggering from the chaos both Wesley brothers had left behind them. John Wesley, especially, had conducted himself with unbending pride, holding himself aloof from the settlers, while trying to force them into his own brand of holiness.

> *Although still in his early twenties, he was the most discussed man in England.*

George, from his experience with the common people of Drummer, reached out to the Savannahians in love and acceptance. He ministered to the soldiers and treated them as equals. They responded to him in love. He preached to everyone: Italians, Germans, Dutch, French, Native Americans as well as the English. Everywhere, people responded to his message of love and grace.

The harsh climate and rugged life of the settlers had robbed many children of parents. On a visit to the Salzberger settlement north of Savannah, Whitefield toured their orphanage—the first in America—and became determined to do the same for Savannah's orphans. He stayed in Georgia four months, only leaving for full ordination as an Anglican priest. In his heart burned the dream for the children along with America's lost souls.

He faced another Wesley upheaval upon his return to England in late 1738. This time, however, he found the country in full revival as the brothers preached from city to city. Along with his riveting preaching, John's organizational skills helped the movement's rapid growth. He organized societies among the converts, printed hymn books and set England aflame.

Kingswood changed George Whitefield for life. Never again would man's opinion concern him.

Whitefield threw himself back into the circuit preaching he had started before his time in Georgia. He was determined to preach to England's most despised, so he traveled to Kingswood to preach to the coal miners there. No clergy would allow use of their churches, so Whitefield took the scandalous step of field preaching. On Saturday, February 17, 1739, he donned a clerical robe and wig, marched to a nearby hill and delivered his first outdoor message.

On this day, silent, coal-blackened faces turned up to hear this novelty before them—a slight, young man with one squinty eye. The priest opened his sermon with a joke. *First shock.* He used illustrative stories they understood. *Second shock.* He spoke of a God who cared about them—the nobodies of British society—a God who loved them; who longed for a relationship with them. Pink rivers flowed from tears cutting through the coal dust. The people repented, embraced Whitefield's God and broke out into singing.

Kingswood changed George Whitefield for life. Never again would man's opinion concern him. He preached where he wanted, how he wanted, to whom he wanted, causing an uproar in organized religion. Thousands gathered to hear him preach every day and sometimes several times in a day. When he learned of needs among the people, such as a school, he raised the funds to build one.

He resolved to preach in the most godless city of the time—London. He would preach to the most disdained, so he headed to Moorfields, where common people congregated for fun. After delivering a fiery message there, he moved on to Kennington Common where folks gathered to watch public executions. Standing next to the scaffold, he delivered a message to 30,000. He preached to over 80,000 in Hyde Park over the next few months. One witness wrote, "The more the Pharisees roar, the more the crowds soar." By the age of 24, George Whitefield was the most famous man in England.

Like the Wesleys, he organized the new converts into societies. He raised funds to build schools, feed the poor and set money aside for the orphans in Georgia. He returned to America in 1739, determined to bring revival across the ocean. He chose Philadelphia, then the largest city of the colonies.

Benjamin Franklin, the skeptic, came to hear him speak.

Benjamin Franklin, the skeptic, came to hear him speak. He marveled at Whitefield's voice as he preached along the river. Curious as to how far it traveled, he walked 12 blocks, until he ceased hearing each word. Through simple math computation, Franklin deduced that Whitefield could successfully preach to at least 35,000 people at one time. Another eyewitness wrote, he was "the best show in town with eternal consequences."

Although Whitefield abhorred the treatment of slaves, he did not condemn the institution itself. He believed the Blacks possessed souls, while most others did not. Therefore, he preached to the Blacks, while encouraging their masters to take an interest in their souls. He also urged more humane treatment. Although

Georgia was the only colony which specifically banned slavery at its founding, he later compromised and spoke publicly in favor of it in order to use the additional manpower to build his coming orphanage, which he named Bethesda (House of Mercy). It is still in operation today as a boys' school.

Seven times George Whitefield traveled to America. He preached up and down the entire Atlantic seaboard. He believed the land was marked by God and called her a "City on a Hill." The Anglican Church in England took steps to dominate American life. From his many years in the colonies, Whitefield knew the Americans would never submit to the stringency of the mother church. He sounded the alarm both in America and in England. Colonists caught his vision. They began moving toward the unthinkable—self-governance. Even the Patriots took notice (Sam Adams, George Washington, Patrick Henry). He inspired them to consider a government apart from the church. Although he died before the Revolution, George Whitefield played a major role in the vision for true independence.

George Whitefield died in Newberry, Connecticut when he was only 56 years old. Constant preaching destroyed his health. However, he would remark to those who urged him to slow down that it was "better to wear out rather than rust out." At the time of his death, he was the most famous, most loved and most hated man of his day. He'd crossed the ocean 13 times to bring the Good News to America and to raise funds for his beloved orphans. He cared nothing for a legacy. In his own words: "Let the name of George Whitefield perish so long as the name of Christ is exalted."

PART 3

THE SLAVES

—George Liele
(ca. 1750 – 1828)

Photo courtesy of Derrek Curry, Executive Director of George Leile Visions, INC. Taken of portrait which hangs in the museum of the First African Baptist Church

CHAPTER 6

GEORGE LIELE

George Liele was born in Virginia, circa 1750. His parents, Liele and Nancy were enslaved. George Liele was sold to Henry Sharpe at such a young age, he had no memories of either parents. Later, people told him his father was a "God Fearing" man.

Many white owners forced their slaves to attend church; not for salvation but for the preacher to berate them into submissive obedience. Liele's owner was unique. Not only did he believe his slaves possessed souls, he encouraged them to be baptized upon conversion. After a move to the Georgia frontier, he contacted his brother-in-law to lead a congregation in his own home until a church building could be built. Liele became a believer at the age of 23 years old.

The joy he experienced upon conversion inspired him to talk to the other slaves. Henry Sharpe learned of this and gave Liele a Bible. He had encouraged his slaves to learn to read and write, despite laws against it. Shortly after this, he and Pastor Moore asked Liele to preach to the mixed congregation. Afterwards, the Whites voted unanimously to ordain him, making him the first ordained Black man in the colonies. Sharpe gave Liele the freedom to ride from plantation to plantation, preaching to his people. While at Silver Bluff (15 miles south of Augusta, Georgia, on the Savannah River and owned by George Galphin), Liele reunited with his childhood friend, David George.

George Liele loved to preach on God's liberation of his chosen people from the Egyptians. His special chapter was Psalm 68. He gave hope to his hopeless race. Had not God heard the cries of His people and rescued them? He would do the same for the enslaved Africans.

The first time George Liele preached at Silver Bluff, he chose to read Matthew 11:28-29. "Come unto me, all ye that labor and are heavy-laden, and I will give you rest. Take my yoke upon you and learn of me, for I am meek and lowly and ye shall find rest for your souls" (Matthew 11:28-29 KJV). After preaching his message, David George approached him, telling him of his own recent conversion experience.

> *Before assuming active duty, he granted Liele his freedom.*

As the American Revolution neared, Liele's master, Henry Sharpe, loyal to the British Crown, moved his family and slaves to British-held Savannah. After his arrival, the British army assigned Sharp a captaincy and sent him to Tybee Island. Sharpe asked Liele to accompany him as a man-servant. Before assuming active duty, he granted Liele his freedom. Liele immediately changed his surname from Sharpe (the custom of the day was for the slave to take on the name of their owner) to Liele, his father's name.

Henry Sharpe died in battle on Tybee Island. His heirs had Liele seized and placed in jail in an attempt to re-enslave him. The authorities released him after he produced legal papers of manumission. He continued preaching to the slaves at nearby plantations, where he met Andrew Bryan, who worked on Brampton Plantation. Later, David George arrived from Silver Bluff. The three men worked together, watching the war with anxious eyes. Liberty for the colonies meant slavery for all three.

The British lost territory after territory. Savannah Loyalists prepared to flee. George Liele met with the British officer in charge of the exodus, Colonel Kirkland. He agreed to pay passage for Liele, his wife and four children to Jamaica, in return for a period of indentured servitude.

Once in Jamaica, the colonel introduced Liele to the governor, General Campbell, who immediately gave Liele work carrying shot (ammunition) from the military base at Port Royal to Kingston, a trip of 30 miles. As he continued in hauling work, Leile prospered enough to buy several slaves of his own to help. He paid off his debt and once again became a free man.

Slave conditions in America had been harsh. In Jamaica, it was horrific. The only Whites on the island were plantation owners. They ruled with brutality. The entire island revolved around plantation life. The freedom to preach that Liele had enjoyed in the colonies did not exist on this island. He was often questioned, forced to write out every sermon and prayer for approval, and rang the bell before and after services, so the owners would know when to expect their slaves to return. Many Blacks felt he catered too much to the Whites, but his desire to keep preaching, under any circumstances, drove him to it. Although a freed man, the government could shut him down at any moment, and he knew it.

Liele wrote to the British Baptist Society, requesting funds to build his first church in Jamaica. Through letters, he met Dr. John Rippon, the secretary general of the organization. They forged a strong friendship through letters. The society funded the two churches Liele planted in Jamaica, which exist to this day.

In 1822, Liele accepted an invitation from Dr. Rippon to minister to London's freed Blacks. He stayed six years and died shortly after his return to Jamaica. Throughout his life, George Liele never lost sight of his life purpose—to preach Christ to everyone, but especially his Black brothers and sisters.

—David George
(1742 – 1810)

Cotton Tree ~ Freetown, Sierra Leone - Photo courtesy of Alfred Kanu

CHAPTER 7

DAVID GEORGE

David fled the Chappell plantation in Virginia after watching his cruel master beat his mother to death. Eventually, he became the property of George Galphin, owner of the Silver Bluff trading post and plantation. This fascinating man had abandoned a wife in Ireland to make his mark in the New World. His fair treatment of the Natives won their loyalty. On his farm, Whites, Blacks and Natives worked together in harmony.

David George lived as wild as any slave could. A visiting Black told him he would never see God's glory if he didn't change his ways. David, illiterate and terrified, began praying the Lord's Prayer. The more he prayed, the worse he felt. After a prolonged period of inner turmoil, he came to understand that God loved him and only wanted to forgive him.

A White itinerant preacher from Connecticut, Wait Palmer, came to preach to the enslaved. After listening to his message, David George asked to be baptized with water. Soon after that, a Black preacher visited the plantation. David George had known George Liele in Virginia. They were pleased to reconnect. George Liele was already literate. David George found an old child's primer and taught himself to read with the help of Galphin's children.

The Galphin trading post lay between Augusta and Savannah. When Savannah fell to the British on December 28, 1779, the planter knew the British would march to Augusta next. Because of his Patriot views, he packed up his family and fled, leaving 50 slaves to fend for themselves. They promptly headed south and east toward Savannah.

Desperate for fighting men on American soil, British Lord

North had issued a proclamation that any enslaved person willing to fight for the king would be immediately freed. Thousands of slaves accepted the invitation (including one of George Washington's own slaves, Harry Washington, up in Virginia). By siding with the British, David George (who took on his friend's name as his own surname) won freedom for himself and his family.

After the American victory over Britain, David George, along with thousands of other Loyalists, sought ways to leave the newly freed colonies. Many chose to accept England's offer to settle in British-held Nova Scotia. The former slaves rejoiced, anticipating a new life in this Promised Land. They sailed north with high hopes. However, rocky soil, long harsh winters, and lack of adequate shelter tested their mettle from the start. Disbanded British soldiers, unaccustomed to losing wars, roamed with liquor in their bodies and frustration in their hearts. They targeted the hapless Black Loyalists, destroyed their rude huts and drove them out of town.

> *The former slaves rejoiced, anticipating a new life in this Promised Land.*

Ten years later, most Black Loyalists jumped at the chance to begin a new settlement on the African continent. A company had formed in London, trying to find a viable solution to the many freed Blacks living in the city. Led by Granville Sharp, the Sierra Leone Company offered free passage to any Black Loyalist wishing to go. They expected 500 to take the offer. More than 1,200 accepted.

When the 15 ships sailed on January 15, 1792, David left behind seven churches, several of which were mixed congregations. Lieutenant John Clarkson, younger brother of one board member, led the pilgrims on the voyage to their new home. The 22 days at sea tested their resolve in new ways. Along with many others, Clarkson fell ill to the point the doctor onboard declared him dead. Moments before sliding the body into the sea, a sailor detected movement and the unconscious leader was carried back to his quarters. Others died in the storm. All cheered when the hills of Sierra Leone (Lion Mountains) appeared. The survivors stepped off the boats and marched to the largest tree available. To this day, the Cotton Tree is a Freetown landmark. Here, the Nova Scotians sang praises and thanked God for their arrival.

New challenges faced them immediately. They had arrived at the onset of the tropical monsoon season. Week after week, they huddled in their makeshift huts and prayed for dry weather. Wild animals killed their small animals. Sometimes, they carried off a child.

Once again, the government lagged in delivering promised land allotments to the Nova Scotians. The Sierra Leone Company, which had provided them with free passage, materials for building, and food for a year, sought to control every aspect of their lives. The settlers struggled for self-governance. As he had many times in his long life, David George stepped between the White and Black peoples to find a way of peace. Some accused him of too much compliance, as had the Jamaicans of George Liele. However, David George, ever the pragmatist, had foresight for what could and what could not win. He burned to preach the Gospel of Jesus Christ.

—Andrew Bryan
(1737 – 1812)

Andrew Bryan, *The history of the Negro church* (Washington, D.C.: Associated Publishers, 1921) by Carter Godwin Woodson

Public Domain Image, Courtesy New York Public Library (b11995308)

CHAPTER 8

ANDREW BRYAN

ndrew Bryan, worked as a driver for Jonathan Bryan. He lived on Brampton Plantation, his master's rice plantation. George Whitefield had preached on this plantation after convincing the owner that slaves possess souls. Andrew Bryan was one of his converts. Jonathan Bryan allowed the slaves to congregate in one of his barns, where Bryan, Liele, and George preached. This became the foundation of what would later be known as the First African Baptist Church on Montgomery Street in Savannah.

David George had fled to Nova Scotia and George Liele to Jamaica after the American Revolution rather than risk re-enslavement. Andrew Bryan chose to remain in Savannah to pastor the flock left behind where he faced much persecution from suspicious Whites. Once, after receiving a brutal beating, he shouted how privileged he was to suffer the same as his Lord and Savior, Jesus Christ.

Later, the son of Jonathan Bryan allowed Andrew Bryan to purchase his own freedom. The church helped him raise the money to free his wife. He bought the property where Bryan Baptist Church sits today. Until the end of his own life in 1812, Bryan would purchase abused slaves, allowing them to work off the cost to gain their own freedom.

PART 4

THE PERSECUTED

9

THE PERSECUTED SALZBURGERS

JOHANN MARTIN BOLZIUS
(1703 – 1765)

FLIGHT OF THE SALZBURGERS
(1734)

"Our Salzburgers did not leave their home for the sake of good living; under the merciful guidance of our miraculous God they landed in this quiet corner of the world in order to strive first and foremost for God's kingdom and His justice."

—JOHANN MARTIN BOLZIUS

CHAPTER 9

THE PERSECUTED SALZBURGERS

The Salzburgers involved peoples of different countries bound together by their Lutheran faith. The name derives from their settling on the Salzach River in modern Austria. They worked in local salt mines. The Catholic archbishops of the region ignored the Lutherans until 1560 when most of Salzburg had converted to their faith. Fearing wealth and power would be lost to the growing Lutheran movement, Catholic bishops pushed back.

Finally, the Archbishop of Salzburg ordered the first expulsion in 1684, forcing adults to leave their children behind as they entered into exile. The second order came in 1686.

Count Leopold Anton Eleutherius von Firmian was elected archbishop of Salzburg in 1727. He was determined to rid the region of all Protestants and targeted the salt miners. He issued an illegal edict—The Edict of Expulsion. Then, he ordered all un-propertied people to leave in eight days. He allowed those owning property to stay three months to sell before leaving.

Frederick William of Brandenburg-Prussia accepted the responsibility of protecting the 20,000 refugees. Many died on the road. This triumphal march of martyrdom inspired other Protestants, who stepped forward to help. England opened her arms to assist them to the New World. She helped other persecuted groups, such as the Huguenots and Waldensians, as well. King George, as Duke of Hanover-Brunswick, participated in the Society for Promoting Christian Knowledge. This society's focus was to bring the gospel to the British poor and the American colonies.

One member, Samuel Urlsperger, was the senior of the Lutheran ministry in Augsburg. A descendant of exiled Austrian Protestants, he assisted the Salzburgers seeking refuge. He worked with The Georgia Board of Trustees to secure passage to the colony. The trustees commissioned Urlsburger to recruit 300 Salzburgers to sail to America; however, most had already settled in Prussia. An English agent persuaded 25 to go to Georgia. More joined. The final group numbered 37. After meeting the new pastors, Bolzius and Gronau, in Rotterdam, the Salzburgers left for their new home.

They met Oglethorpe in Charleston, who was returning to England. He postponed his departure to escort them to Georgia. They sailed up the river to Savannah on March 5, 1734. Benjamin Sheftall, a Jew, met the ship and served the newcomers rice soup. Afterwards, Oglethorpe escorted the newest arrivals to the land he had chosen for them, about 25 miles from Savannah. The Salzburgers named their new town

> *The Salzburgers named their new town Ebenezer (Stone of Help).*

Ebenezer (Stone of Help). Unfortunately, the swamps of the area brought illness. Like Savannahians, the settlers sickened and some died. Because so many children lost both parents to disease, the Salzburgers founded the first orphanage in America to meet their needs.

The second group left Augsburg (Germany), on September 23, 1734. They sailed to England where they met Tomochichi and his entourage. They boarded the *Prince of Wales* and arrived in Georgia on December 28, 1734. The third group sailed with Oglethorpe, the Wesley brothers, and the Moravians.

Bolzius demanded better land for his diminishing flock.

Oglethorpe relocated them to the mouth of Ebenezer Creek at the Savannah River, where they erected their first church. They also opened the first public school in Georgia. Today, only the Jerusalem Church (built 1767 - 1769) remains of the original settlement.

THE PERSECUTED MORAVIANS

COUNT ZINZENDORF
(1700 – 1760))

MORAVIAN SEAL

"I have one passion. It is He, only He. Preach the gospel, die and be forgotten."

—COUNT ZINZENDORF

CHAPTER 10

THE PERSECUTED MORAVIANS

The Moravians had experienced intense religious persecution in their home countries. A wealthy man whose estate lay in Saxony, Germany (close to the Czech border), allowed them to settle on his estate. There, they built a community and named it Herrnhut (The Watch of the Lord).

Count Zinzendorf led about 300 of these people who lived by piety and industry. In 1727, they divided a day into watches and began praying around the clock. This lasted more than 100 years! It birthed in them a desire to take the Gospel of Jesus Christ all over the world. Those who left Herrnhut took everything they owned, never expecting to return. Others sold themselves into slavery to preach to other people in bondage.

When the count learned of the Georgia experiment, promising religious freedom to all, he traveled to England to meet with the Georgia Board of Trustees. There, he negotiated passage for a group of Moravians, whose desire was to preach to the Native Americans.

The first group left England on February 3, 1735. The voyage lasted more than nine weeks, during which time, the passengers experienced a violent storm at sea. The Moravians' calm in the face of certain death is what eventually led to John Wesley's conversion.

The Moravians found 600 people living in Savannah at the time of their arrival. Quickly, they set to work, building their own community, helping others, and keeping their schedule of prayer, study, and singing of hymns each evening. Natives came to listen to them sing, often bearing gifts of meat for the latest Savannahians.

Reverend Spangenberg, one of the Moravian leaders, met with Tomochichi and the Musgroves to establish friendly relations. The Moravians also reached out to the Jewish community. In addition, they hosted the Salzburger pastors, Gronau and Bolzius, whenever business brought them to Savannah. All Savannhians appreciated their work ethic and honesty.

However, their pacifist beliefs soon brought them to grief. Because of the Spanish threat to the South, all able-bodied men in Savannah were required to participate in the night watch. Spangenberg refused. The Trustees had exempted him from this requirement, but the pastor carried no papers as proof. As tensions mounted, the pastor traveled to another Moravian settlement, in Pennsylvania. William Penn, founder of the state, was also a pacifist, a Quaker. Reverend Spangenberg learned the Moravians would face no opposition

> *Reverend Spangenberg, one of the Moravian leaders, met with Tomochichi and the Musgroves to establish friendly relations.*

there, plus have much opportunity to minister to Natives. He began working on having the Georgia Moravians move as soon as they paid off the passage debt to the Georgia Board of Trustees.

A Moravian couple, Peter Rose and his wife, lived among the Lower Creeks. They learned enough language to begin teaching the children, as Tomochichi had requested. Every morning and evening, teachers and students read the Bible and prayed. They taught the children to read. In the afternoon, they tended the garden, a gift from the Natives. However, the Native boys grew restless to fight the Spaniards and quit school.

Though they worked hard, owing nothing to anyone, by February of 1737, the city began demanding all Moravian men to take up arms. They refused. Leaders threatened to burn down their dwellings and kill them all. They still refused. Soon, the Moravians found themselves facing mob violence—exactly what they had escaped in the Old World. They decided the time had come to depart for Pennsylvania.

David Zeisburger, Jr., who had followed his parents to Savannah and then north, later became a missionary to the Native Americans, preaching in both Pennsylvania and Ohio. Others named him, "The Apostle to the Natives."

CONCLUSION

George, particularly Savannah, owes much to the people who walked her streets almost 300 years ago. We honor James Oglethorpe, the young aristocrat with brilliant vision and courage, who forged a refuge for the religious persecuted of Europe, fostered a deep trust with the Native peoples around him, and secured the land from the hostile Spanish in the South.

Tomochichi worked with Oglethorpe for the success of Savannah, working tirelessly for continued friendly relations between his people and the European newcomers. The Musgroves bridged the language gap to aid the two leaders. Especially Mary Musgrove, who often served as a diplomat, smoothing over various misunderstandings between the two people groups, to avoid bloodshed.

The Wesley brothers, while more successful in their native England, paved the way for George Whitefield to come to America, who exploded on the scene. Through his many travels up and down the eastern seaboard, he challenged his listeners to embrace their special place in history and become a *Beacon on a Hill* to inspire others. Such words helped ignite the Great Awakening that culminated in the Revolutionary War.

The formerly enslaved George Leile, David George, and Andrew Bryan all lived their God-given destiny despite much prejudice and hardship. All remained shining testaments of God's indomitable power and endless grace throughout their lives. The Salzburgers, Jews, and Moravians all added their own unique religious determination and work ethic. All these and others, served to make Georgia a unique land of diverse cultures, people groups, and aspirations. Georgia—a state visited, lived in, and loved by many.

TIMELINE OF EVENTS

1565
• Spanish founding of St. Augustine

1644 (approximate date)
• Tomochichi born

1670
• Charlestown founded by British

1696
• Oglethorpe born

1700
• Mary Griffin (Musgrove) born in Coweta Town

1703
• John Wesley born

1707
• Charles Wesley born

1709
• Mary Griffin moves to English South Carolina

1715 – 17
• Yamasee War
• Mary Griffin's father murdered

1717
• Mary Griffin marries John Musgrove
• Oglethorpe becomes aide to Eugene, Prince of Savoy, who ends
  Turkish aggression at the Battle of Belgrade

1722
• Oglethorpe elected to the House of Commons
• Oglethorpe leads debtor prison reform

1728
- Tomochichi forms a new tribe and settles on Yamacraw Bluff 1731
- Salzburgers expelled by the Archbishop

1732
- Georgia Trustees granted a charter from King George II
- Trustees offer asylum to the Salzburgers
- Musgroves build trading post on the Savannah River 1733

- **February**
  o Oglethorpe lands in Georgia with 114 settlers
  o Oglethorpe meets with Tomochichi and the Musgroves

- **May**
  o Articles of Friendship signed by Oglethorpe (Britain) and Tomochichi (Lower Creek Nations)

- **July**
  o Georgia's first Thanksgiving
  o First Jews arrive

1734
- First Salzburgers arrive
- Tomochichi and entourage visit England
- First Sunday School (Ebenezer)

1735
- Highlanders arrive and found Darien
- First sawmill in Georgia (Salzburgers)
- John Musgrove and both sons die

1736
- Oglethorpe's second return to Georgia
- Second group of Moravians arrive
- John and Charles Wesley arrive
- Charles Wesley returns to England (after four months in Georgia)
- Andrew Bryan born
- Salzburgers relocate to New Ebenezer
- Moravians start school for Native children

1737
• John Wesley returns to England (After one year in Georgia)
• First orphanage – Ebenezer
• Mary Musgrove marries Jacob Mathewes

1738
• Renewed hostilities between Spain and Britain
• Oglethorpe returns to America with a regiment
• Oglethorpe fortifies Georgia's coastline
• George Whitefield arrives in Savannah
• Charles Wesley is radically saved
• John Wesley is radically saved

1739
• The War of Jenkin's Ear
• Oglethorpe travels inland to strengthen ties with Creek natives
• Tomochichi dies

1740
• Oglethorpe attacks the Spanish fort at St. Augustine (ends in failure)
• First rice and grist mills in Georgia (Salzburgers)

1742
• Spanish invasion of Georgia
• Battle of Bloody Marsh – ends Spanish threat
• David George is born
• Jacob Mathewes die

1743
• Mary Musgrove marries Thomas Bosomworth
• Oglethorpe returns to England the final time

1748
• Treaty to end King George's war (aka War of Jenkins's Ear)

1750
• George Liele is born

1752
- Georgia becomes a royal colony
- Georgia Board of Trustees is dissolved

1765
- Mary Musgrove Mathewes Bosomworth dies

1767-69
- New Jerusalem church built in Ebenezer

1770
- George Whitefield dies in Newburyport, Province of Massachusetts Bay (Age 55)

1777
- First Georgia governor – Adam Treutlen born at Ebenezer

1775-1781
- American Revolution
- George Liele's former master dies on Tybee Island
- George Liele remains in Savannah as a freedman

1778
- Savannah falls to the British
- Ebenezer under British occupation
- David George and 50 slaves escape to British lines

1781
- Oglethorpe learns of American Independence

1782
- David George sails to Nova Scotia with other Black Loyalists

1783
- George Liele baptizes Andrew Bryan in Savannah
- Liele sails to Jamaica

1785
- Oglethorpe meets John Adams
- Oglethorpe dies

1788
• Charles Wesley dies in England (80 years old)

1790
• Andrew Bryan purchases his freedom
• Andrew Bryan purchases his first property to build a church

1791
• John Wesley dies in England (87 years old)

1792
• David George and most Black Loyalists sail to Sierra Leone to
  begin new colony

1810
• David George dies in Sierra Leone

1812
• Andrew Bryan dies in Savannah

1820
• George Liele dies in Jamaica

BIBLIOGRAPHY

A Methodist Preacher. (1903). John Wesley The Methodist New York: The Methodist Book Concern. 319.

Blackburn, Joyce. (1970) James Edward Oglethorpe. Nashville: Cumberland House Publishing. 178.

Fries, Adelaide L. (reprint 1967). The Moravians In Georgia. Baltimore: Genealogical Publishing Company. 252.

Gordon, Grant. (1992). From Slavery to Freedom, The Life of David George, Pioneer Black Baptist Minister. Hantsport: Lancelot Press. 356.

Hahn, Steven C. (2012). The Life and Times of Mary Musgrove. Gainesville: University Press of Florida. 284.

Harrison, G Elsie. (1938) Son to Susanna The Private Life of John Wesley. Nashville: Cokesbury Press. 377.

Jandrlich, Michael. (1990) Andrew Bryan. Retrieved on 10/20/19: https://digitalcommons.georgiasouthern.edu/cgi/viewcontent. cgi?article=1024&context=sav-bios-lane

Jones, Jr., Charles C. (1868-reprint 1998). Historical Sketch of Tomochichi, Mico of the Yamacraws. Savannah: The Oglethorpe Press, Inc. 133.

Jones, George Fenwick. (1997) The Salzburger Saga, Religious Exiles and Other Germans along the Savannah. Rockport: Picton Press. 224.

Mansfield, Stephen. (2001) Forgotten Founding Father. Nashville: Cumberland House. 283.

Renfro, Betty Ford. (2002) River to River, From the Savannah River to the Ogeechee River, The History of Effingham County. Springfield: Historic Effingham Society, Inc. 470.

Schama, Simon. (2006). Rough Crossings, The Slaves, the British, and the American Revolution. New York: HarperCollins Publishers. 478.

Schlesinger, Jr., Arthur M. (2001) James Oglethorpe, Humanitarian and Soldier. East Bridgewater: Chelsea House Publishers. 79.

Shannon, David T. (2012). George Liele's Life and Legacy, An Unsung Hero. Macon: Mercer University Press. 184.

Spalding, Phinizy and Jackson, Edwin. (1988) James Edward Oglethorpe, A New Look at Georgia's founder. Athens: Carl Vinson Institute of Government.33.

For more information and reading:

Mighty Oaks by Arlene Angwin

https://booklocker.com/books/11270.html

You can also contact Arlene at scribeforchrist@gmail.com

Rebecca Bishopriggs, Editor

rlbishopriggs@gmail.com

Holy Ghost Tours - Savannah

Guides relate stories of those individuals featured
in *Foundation Forces*

https://www.holyghosttourssav.com

Spiritual Archaeology: Committed to discovering
Savannah's spiritual roots

spiritualarchaeology.org@gmail.com